Mathematics and Computing/Technology
An Inter-faculty Second Level Course

MT262 Putting Computer Systems to Work

Block I
Beginnings

Unit 3
Looping and Branching

Prepared for the Course Team by Alan Best

This text forms part of the Open University second-level course MT262 *Putting Computer Systems to Work*, which among other things teaches the use of Borland C^{++}Builder 5 Standard to tackle small programming projects. (Borland C^{++}Builder 5 Standard is copyright © 2000 Borland International (UK) Limited.)

The course software comprises the Borland C^{++}Builder 5 Standard CD-ROM and the MT262 Templates and Libraries CD-ROM, both of which are supplied as part of the course.

This publication forms part of an Open University course. Details of this and other Open University courses can be obtained from the Call Centre, PO Box 724, The Open University, Milton Keynes, MK7 6ZS, United Kingdom: tel. +44 (0)1908 653231, e-mail ces-gen@open.ac.uk

Alternatively, you may visit the Open University website at http://www.open.ac.uk where you can learn more about the wide range of courses and packs offered at all levels by the Open University.

To purchase this publication or other components of Open University courses, contact Open University Worldwide Ltd, The Berrill Building, Walton Hall, Milton Keynes, MK7 6AA, United Kingdom: tel. +44 (0)1908 858785, fax +44 (0)1908 858787, e-mail ouwenq@open.ac.uk or website http://www.ouw.co.uk

The Open University, Walton Hall, Milton Keynes, MK7 6AA.

First published 1999. Second edition 2002.

Edited, designed and typeset by The Open University, using the Open University TEX System.

Printed by Henry Ling Limited, Dorchester, Dorset.

ISBN 0 7492 5530 7

2.1

Contents

Introduction   **4**

1 Sequence, selection and iteration   **5**
    1.1   Sequence   5
    1.2   Selection   6
    1.3   Iteration   9

2 Calculator simulation   **11**
    2.1   Designing a solution   12
    2.2   Coding the solution   17
    2.3   Implementing the solution   20

3 Strings   **21**
    3.1   Operations on strings   22
    3.2   String indexes   23

4 Two problems   **26**
    4.1   A first design   26
    4.2   Improving the solution   30
    4.3   Testing the solution   32
    4.4   An extension problem   33

Solutions to the Exercises   **37**

Solutions to the Computer Activities   **47**

Index   **48**

Study guide

A recommended study pattern, based on an average overall study time, is as follows.

Material	Study time
Introduction, Section 1 (text)	2 hours
Section 2 (computer)	3 hours
Section 3 (text)	$1\frac{1}{2}$ hours
Subsections 4.1–4.3 (computer)	$3\frac{1}{2}$ hours
Subsection 4.4 (computer)	$1\frac{1}{2}$ hours

You will need access to your computer whilst studying Sections 2 and 4.

Logically, the whole of Section 4 belongs together, so you may wish to study it in *one* study session. Alternatively, you might find it more convenient to do the design work on the two problems in Section 4 in one session and the two computer activities in another.

You will find it useful to have *Unit 2* or the Handbook available for reference during your study of this unit.

Introduction

The processing power of the computer systems with which this course is concerned comes from one or more microprocessors. These devices, first produced in the 1970s, are mostly intended to carry out instructions in the order in which they are stored in memory. Two things can disturb this orderly obeying of instructions: the instruction being obeyed can itself cause the next instruction to be out of sequence, or an external event can interrupt the flow. The alteration of order caused by external events will not be a direct concern of this course.

This course will be concerned with the consequences of the order in which instructions are normally obeyed, and the fact that instructions can alter the order. Most high-level programming languages provide facilities based on the ability to obey instructions out of the natural order, and you have already exploited some of these in C++ by using **if** and **while** instructions.

The main aims of this unit are to consolidate the various design and coding ideas that you have met, and to give you further practice at using them.

In *Unit 2* you designed, and coded, your first computer programs. This unit continues the development of your understanding and experience of program design. You will be exposed to more complex problems whose solutions force the introduction of further data types and further design constructs.

During your study of *Unit 2* you met four of the basic data types, namely integer, real, character and boolean. You also met string constants. The

4

string data type is arguably the most used of all in computing, and this unit begins a detailed study of strings and their properties, and the standard operations on strings.

Section 1 reviews the design and coding constructs that you have already met, and places them in a slightly more general context. It also introduces some new design ideas that make solutions much more readable.

Section 2 gives practice at designing a solution to a problem, using the new ideas from Section 1. You are also asked to implement the design as a C++ program.

Section 3 returns to the more general level and considers string data. Surprisingly, in view of how much string data is manipulated by desktop PCs and other systems, C and some other languages do not have a specific string data type. This lack has been remedied in a number of different ways by different library suppliers; the Borland provision is discussed here.

Finally, Section 4 gives design and coding practice in two problems involving string data.

1 Sequence, selection and iteration

In *Unit 2* several versions of one main problem were pursued. The progression was rather hasty, rarely stopping to reflect on what had been done; nor was any attempt made to pull together strategies that could be made more general. This section begins to put that right by reviewing, and consolidating, some important notions which have been encountered.

In building up any design for a solution, and subsequently any computer implementation to a problem, there are three basic concepts that will appear repeatedly. They are known as *sequence, selection* and *iteration*. Each is discussed in turn. They form the basis of what is often called **structured programming**. Used carefully, they enable readable and maintainable code to be developed.

1.1 Sequence

Ever since the advent of the microprocessor in the 1970s, computer systems have been constructed using one or more of these processing units. Each individual processor is a sequential device, in the sense that it carries out instructions in the order in which they are held in memory unless the instruction being obeyed tells it to do otherwise. Although modern systems may well have a number of processors, each carrying out a task, individual tasks are normally designed and coded taking this sequential basis for granted. Where a single task is genuinely shared between several processors, different design and programming techniques are required that are beyond the scope of this course.

Your desktop PC can simultaneously transfer data from the hard disk and carry out operations on data stored in memory.

The way in which the steps in a design have been presented acknowledges the sequential nature of designs. The steps are numbered and are to be thought of as being carried out in numerical order unless a **loop** or **if** step is encountered. It is this ordering of design (and code) steps that is referred to as the concept of **sequence**.

Sequence is a simple idea, but vital. For instance, the following design for a program to add VAT (at 17.5%) to an amount entered from the keyboard involves just four steps. The four steps must be carried out in the given sequence; any reordering of them would invalidate the design. The variables *Amount* and *WithVat* are both of type real.

1   write out "Enter the amount: "
2   read in *Amount*
3   *WithVat* ← *Amount* * 1.175
4   write out "With VAT added that becomes ", *WithVat*

Note that step 4 combines two write out steps. Putting it this way acknowledges how such steps are coded using one of the various *Write* facilities, as you have seen in *Unit 2*. This design practice will be used where appropriate.

If a design (or program) is purely sequential, with no loops, it might be thought to be very limited; the above VAT design is not very versatile. If only console application programs are being used, purely sequential designs *are* very limited. However, event-driven *Windows* programs, which are developed in Blocks III and IV, typically consist of a large number of small pieces of code, many of which consist of a short sequence of instructions. The versatility of *Windows* programs comes from the variety of ways in which such pieces of code are used, via menus, buttons, etc. (Loops and other non-sequential code are still involved, but occur in the operating system rather than the program that you write.)

1.2 Selection

In the work that you have already done, you have met the need to carry out different actions depending on, say, what the user has provided as input. The general concept of following different paths through a design (or program) according to some criterion, is called **selection**. All languages of the type represented by C and C^{++} provide a number of selection methods. The one that you have met is the **if** selection process where one of two paths is followed depending on whether a condition is true or false.

Selection, or branching, is a key concept in designing for C^{++}-type languages.

In designs, the **if** selection step takes the following form.

> **if** condition **then**
>   carry out **then** actions
> **else**
>   carry out **else** actions
> **ifend**

The boolean value of the condition selects which of the two branches of this design is to be followed. But whichever branch is selected, whether the **then** actions or the **else** actions are carried out, on completion the design moves on to the next step in sequence, that is, to whatever comes immediately after the **ifend**.

The steps in a design must be numbered sequentially. When, as here, a *fragment* of a design is given, the numbering is somewhat arbitrary, so the numbers are omitted.

You have also seen a design example showing that **if** steps can be nested. Either or both of the **then** and **else** actions can themselves involve selection, thereby allowing the sequence to branch in more than two ways. Try the following two exercises on nested **if** steps.

Unit 2, Exercise 3.5

Exercise 1.1 _____

Complete the following **if** step to give four different courses of action depending on the colour of traffic lights namely: if red, stop; if green, go; if amber, stop if safe (to do so); if red and amber, prepare to go.

> **if** lights are red **then**
>> stop
>
> **else**
>> ⋮
>
> **ifend**

You need not number the steps, but do take care with the indentation of your design — it should be clear which actions belong to which **then** or **else**.

Regard 'red and amber' as being a fourth colour.

Exercise 1.2 _____

The table below gives the (hypothetical) insurance premium in pounds for two types of car and two categories of driver.

	Saloon	Sports car
Under 25	360	520
25 and over	290	440

Complete the details of the following **if** step, in which *Premium* (in pounds) is an integer variable, to capture the information given in the table. (For the purposes of this exercise, a car is either a saloon or a sports car.)

> **if** type of car is saloon **then**
>> **if** age of driver is under 25 **then**
>>> *Premium* ← 360
>>
>> **else**
>>> ⋮
>>
>> **ifend**
>
> **else**
>> ⋮
>
> **ifend**

[*Solutions on page 37*]

_____

The ability to nest **if** steps is very useful but, as you can see from the first of the above exercises, the design quickly becomes cumbersome when you start nesting to any non-trivial depths. In executing the design in the solution to Exercise 1.1, first the condition 'lights are red' is examined and the path through the step branches according to the boolean value of the condition. If it has value false, the **else** branch is selected, whereupon the condition 'lights are green' is evaluated. If this condition too is false, you move on to evaluate the condition 'lights are amber'. So you might have to evaluate all these three conditions in finding your path through the nested **if** step; this seems inefficient. As all four colours for the lights are known, would it not be possible to go directly to the appropriate actions? In fact, this *is* possible.

There is another selection construct that expresses a nested **if** in a simplified format: the **case** step. Using this, the solution to Exercise 1.1 would be as follows.

> **select case** depending on colour of lights
> > red: stop
> > green: go
> > amber: stop if safe
> > red and amber: prepare to go
>
> **selectend**

Between the markers **select** and **selectend** are listed pairs consisting of a possible colour of the lights together with the appropriate action to be taken. Which action is selected depends on the current colour of the lights.

The general format of the design **case** step is as follows.

> **select case** depending on value of expression
> > value 1 : actions appropriate to value 1
> > value 2 : actions appropriate to value 2
> > $\vdots$
> > value n : actions appropriate to value n
>
> **else**
> > default action
>
> **selectend**

The expression mentioned in the first line is called the **selector**, and can be anything which yields an appropriate value. For instance, it might be the current value of some variable, or the result of some calculation. There follows a list of possible values that the selector can take, called **case labels**, together with the appropriate actions to be taken should that case arise. When the **case** step is carried out, the current value of the selector determines, by means of the appropriate case label, which set of actions to follow.

The list of case labels need not cover all possible values of the selector. To cater for this there is an optional 'catch-all' **default action**, listed in an **else** part. For any value of the selector that does not appear in the case labels, it is the default action that is carried out. This facility is most useful when there is the possibility of unexpected values of the selector.

In the design, note the colon between each value of the selector and the associated action.

In most actual languages there are restrictions on the types of value that the selector can take. The restrictions for C++ will be discussed later.

Exercise 1.3 ─────────────────────────

A program concerned with analysing text entered from the keyboard keeps count of how many of each of the five vowels have been keyed in, together with a count of how many non-vowels have been keyed in.

Complete the design of the following **case** step whose purpose is to update the appropriate count. (Assume that all characters are entered in lower-case.)

> read in next character from keyboard
> **select case** depending on character
> > 'a' : add 1 to count of a's
> > $\vdots$
>
> **selectend**

[*Solution on page 38*]

In general, the default part of a **case** step is optional. In the traffic lights example no default option was specified, the reason being that all combinations of traffic light colours were dealt with in the case labels. (The traffic lights were assumed to be working correctly, and alternatives such as flashing amber lights were ignored.) For completeness, 'else do nothing' could have been added as a default part to this **case** step. From now on, the instructions to do nothing in the **else** option of either a **case** or an **if** step will usually be omitted. For example, for the following shortened form of the **if** step

> **if** condition **then**
> > carry out **then** actions
>
> **ifend**

it is to be assumed that when the condition evaluates to false (which would normally invoke the **else** actions), no actions are carried out.

You will get more practice with selection and learn how to code the **case** step very shortly, but first iteration, the final member of the trilogy of basic concepts, is discussed.

The **ifend** and **selectend** must never be omitted in design as these are important markers of the end of the construct.

1.3 Iteration

Many of the problems for which computers are used require the same processes to be applied to large volumes of data. Thus the same (often short) sequence of steps has to be repeated over and over again.

This process of repeating a sequence of steps is called **iteration**. In design and coding, loops are used for iteration. You have already met one loop construct, the **while** loop, in *Unit 2*; it has the following general form.

Looping is a key concept in designing for C^{++}-type languages.

> **loop while** condition (is true)
> > steps of loop body
>
> **loopend**

A **while** loop is one type of **conditioned loop**. If, on reaching the loop control step the (boolean) value of the condition is true, then the loop body is entered; if the condition is false, then the loop body is by-passed, i.e. the loop body is not entered. The loop body having been entered, execution continues round and round the steps of the loop body until some step within the loop body causes the loop condition to change to false. Thus it is not known in advance how many times a loop is going to be iterated.

You may well have spotted a potential source of errors in **while** loops: if the loop is entered and nothing in the loop body ever makes the condition false, then the loop will try to execute forever.

There is a second, very similar, type of conditioned loop: the **when** loop. The difference is that the control condition is placed at the completion of the loop body rather than at entry. It takes the following form.

> **loop**
> > steps of loop body
> **loopend when** condition (is true)

Iteration ends when the condition becomes true. For example, the following fragment of design (which employs a character variable *NextChar*) repeatedly asks for characters to be typed from the keyboard until a capital letter is entered.

> **loop**
> > write out "Enter a character: "
> > read in *NextChar*
> **loopend when** *NextChar* lies in range 'A' to 'Z'

The **while** loop is known as a **pre-conditioned loop**, because the condition is tested prior to entry to the loop body. In contrast, the **when** loop is an example of a **post-conditioned loop**, for which the condition is tested on completion of the loop body. These two kinds of loop are very similar and can often be used almost interchangably. This is illustrated in the next exercise.

Exercise 1.4 _____

Convert the above example of a post-conditioned loop into a pre-conditioned loop. That is, design a **while** loop whose purpose is to receive a character entered from the keyboard, until a capital letter is entered.

What differences, if any, do you observe between the two designs?

[*Solution on page 38*]

_____

The main, but subtle, difference between the two types of conditioned loop is the following. In a post-conditioned loop, the **when** loop body is always carried out at least once. The sequence of steps passes through the loop body once before the loop control condition is tested for the first time. In contrast, if the loop control condition in a pre-conditioned loop is false on first arrival, then the **while** loop will be iterated zero times. This difference is one of which designers can often take advantage — for example, to avoid initialisation.

The C++ code for **when** loops will be introduced shortly. For the moment, here is one more design exercise involving a **when** loop.

Exercise 1.5 _____

Consider the following design, in which *Next* and *First* are integer variables.

```
1     read in First
2     Next ← First
3     loop
4        write out Next
5        if Next is odd then
6           Next ← 3 * Next − 1
7        else
8           Next ← Next/2
9        ifend
10    loopend when Next ≤ First
```

What is written out when each of the following values is entered at step 1 as the value of *First*?

(a) 5   (b) 6   (c) 9

[*Solution on page 38*]

_____

There is one further kind of loop that this course will use. This type of loop executes a *pre-determined* number of times, no matter what changes take place while the iteration is going on. For example, a program analysing the numbers obtained from 1000 rolls of a die would probably involve a loop which iterated 1000 times. Something to be carried out for each of 22 pupils in a school class might involve a loop executing 22 times (once for each pupil). An account of this loop — the **for** loop, which is unconditioned — will be postponed until Block II. In the meantime, the two conditioned loops provide plenty of scope.

You may care to note that 'goto' statements, which exist in some languages, have not been used. The 'goto' statement offers the possibility of jumping around in code in ways that make tracing the execution of code extremely difficult. There is a classic paper by the pioneer E. W. Dijkstra which explains the problems.

It may be found in *Communications of the ACM*, March 1968, pp 147–8.

2 Calculator simulation

In this section the design and coding of a solution to the following problem is discussed. The solution will involve some of the new ideas just encountered.

Problem Specification   Calculator simulation

A program is required which is to simulate computations carried out on a certain type of simple pocket calculator, as follows. The user enters a first value. Then the user enters an operator — which can be + (addition), or − (subtraction), or * (multiplication), or / (division) — followed by an operand (second value). (The entering of an operator and an operand can be repeated any number of times.) The operation is carried out on the current value and the operand, the answer becoming the revised current value. When the '=' key is pressed instead of one of the four operators, the result of the calculation is to be output.   □

2.1   Designing a solution

Is the problem specification clear? To illustrate the type of calculation envisaged, consider the following sequence of keypresses.

$7/3*11 + 4*2 =$

This means (on this calculator) that 7 is to be divided by 3, the answer to this is multiplied by 11, 4 is then added to the running answer, and finally this is multiplied by 2. The '=' completes the task, calling for the final answer to be written on the calculator display. The specification suggests that a design to carry out single calculations of this sort is required, with the data under the control of the user.

The specification does not say what types of numbers are to be expected or accepted. A reasonable first assumption is that they are real numbers, particularly as division generally does not yield a whole number as answer.

Having tidied up the specification a little, the next stage is a top-level design. There is going to be a single overall calculation involving any number of operations. The calculation will require a loop. The number of iterations is not known in advance, being under the control of the user when the program is running. This means that a conditioned (**while** or **when**) loop is appropriate. The decision on which type of loop to use is, in general, not taken at the first design stage at which a loop appears — one type may be seen to be more appropriate as the design unfolds. To make progress, it is convenient to write loops initially as **while** loops. (If it turns out that a **when** loop is required, then the design is modified accordingly.)

As in earlier designs, some initialisations are likely to be needed before entering the loop. Thus the following top-level design includes all the main features.

1   initialise variables
2   **loop while** there are more operations to carry out
3   carry out next operation
4   **loopend**
5   write out final answer

In order to do a first refinement of this top-level design, you need to consider the variables involved.

Exercise 2.1 _____

Identify three variables which are going to be needed in the design.
Construct a preliminary data table.

[Solution on page 39]

_____

In theory, now that there is a preliminary data table, the initialisation
(step 1) could be refined to incorporate the data table decisions. In fact, it
is often wise to postpone decisions about initialisation. The basic reason
for this advice is that a decision has not yet been made about the type of
conditioned loop to be used. As pointed out earlier, with a **while** loop the
control condition is checked before the loop is entered: any variable used in
the loop condition must have a value at this point and needs to be
initialised. In contrast, if a **when** loop is used, then the condition is
checked at the end and the variables involved usually acquire values in the
body of the loop, so initialisation before the loop may well be unnecessary.
Although 'extra' initialisation is harmless from the point of view of the
eventual program, for the sake of readability, it is a good idea not to
include unnecessary code. For these reasons, the loop is discussed next.

The way in which step 2 of the top-level design is worded

2   **loop while** there are more operations to carry out

suggests the use of a pre-conditioned **while** loop, but a post-conditioned
when loop is a feasible alternative. In either case, the condition that stops
the loop *is* known: when the '=' key is pressed, the loop should terminate.

This discussion suggests two ways of refining steps 2 and 4 either as a
pre-conditioned loop

2.1   **loop while** *Operator* ≠ '='   *Operator* will require
3   . . .   initialisation in this version.
4   **loopend**

or as a post-conditioned loop

2.1   **loop**
3   . . .
4.1   **loopend when** *Operator* = '='   *Operator* will not require
                                                  initialisation in this version; it
The decision on which type of loop to use will be taken together with the   will acquire a value in the
refinement of the loop body, step 3. (Some possibilities are presented in the loop before being used.
next exercise.) In each pass round the loop, three things must happen: an
operator is read in, a value is read in, and a revised value for the answer is
calculated. It is now necessary to decide how to place entry and testing in   A discussion of the case when
the loop.   the operator is '=' is given in
                                                                               the solution to the next
                                                                               exercise.

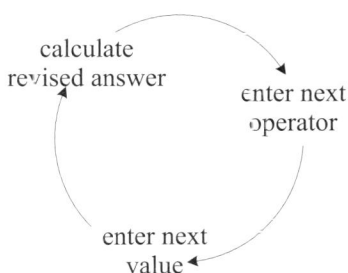

calculate
revised answer   enter next
                        operator

            enter next
              value

13

Some of the various possible ways of refining steps 2, 3 and 4 are listed in the next exercise.

Exercise 2.2 _____

Consider the following alternative refinements of steps 2, 3 and 4. Which one would you choose? (Note that step 1, which must deal with setting up whichever loop is chosen, has still to be refined.)

(a) 2.1 **loop while** *Operator* ≠ '='
    3.1   read in *Operator*
    3.2   read in *NextVal*
    3.3   update *Answer*
    4   **loopend**

(b) 2.1 **loop**
    3.1   read in *Operator*
    3.2   read in *NextVal*
    3.3   update *Answer*
    4.1   **loopend when** *Operator* = '='

(c) 2.1 **loop while** *Operator* ≠ '='
    3.1   read in *NextVal*
    3.2   update *Answer*
    3.3   read in *Operator*
    4   **loopend**

(d) 2.1 **loop**
    3.1   read in *NextVal*
    3.2   update *Answer*
    3.3   read in *Operator*
    4.1   **loopend when** *Operator* = '='

[*Solution on page 39*]

_____

As the discussion in the solution to Exercise 2.2 indicated, the choice between options (c) and (d) is mainly a matter of personal preference. The course team has chosen to pursue option (d) in order to illustrate a post-conditioned loop and, eventually, its coding. (You might wish to think about the consequences of choosing option (c).)

In option (d), the operator to be applied next is read in at step 3.3. If it is '=', then the loop halts immediately. If it is one of the four arithmetic operators, then the loop is repeated and the value of the operator just obtained will be used in the calculation in step 3.2 next time round. That seems to be just what is wanted. A word of caution is in order: the appropriate initialisation must be done so that the loop will act correctly the first time through.

Most languages like C++ have a construct for implementing a (post-conditioned) **when** loop, but some do not.

14

Exercise 2.3

Refine steps 1 and 5 of the original top-level design, using option (d) of Exercise 2.2, to complete a first refinement of that design. For step 1 you will need to decide which of the three variables require initialisation, and to what values.

[*Solution on page 40*]

The design is making good progress. Text is needed for prompts and messages in the *read in* and *write out* steps. There is one other step which needs more work before the design could be considered as final, namely step 3.2. When step 3.2 is encountered, *Answer*, *NextVal* and *Operator* will all have values, and the value of *Answer* needs to be revised accordingly. The loop control guarantees that the value of *Operator* is not '=' at this time, so (assuming that the user has not hit any illegal keys at step 3.3!) *Operator* must have one of the values '+', '−', '*' or '/'. Different calculations are involved, depending on this value. This situation suggests the use of a **case** step.

3.2.1 **select case** depending on *Operator*
3.2.2 '+' : *Answer* ← *Answer* + *NextVal*
3.2.3 '−' : *Answer* ← *Answer* − *NextVal*
3.2.4 '*' : *Answer* ← *Answer* * *NextVal*
3.2.5 '/' : *Answer* ← *Answer*/*NextVal*
3.2.6 **else**
3.2.7   write out "Error! Enter last operator and number again."
3.2.8 **selectend**

The case of *NextVal* having value zero in step 3.2.5 is discussed below.

The way in which the **else** part has been used is worth noting. If the value last entered for the operator is not one of the permissible four, no calculation takes place. The user is warned of this and the design moves on in sequence to the entry of another operator (step 3.3) and value (step 3.1).

Thus the **else** part has helped to include a simple form of error-trapping.

A little work on steps 3.1, 3.3 and 5.1 yields the following final design.

1.1 *Answer* ← 0
1.2 *Operator* ← '+'
2.1 **loop**
3.1.1 write out "Enter next number: "
3.1.2 read in *NextVal*
3.2.1 **select case** depending on *Operator*
3.2.2   '+' : *Answer* ← *Answer* + *NextVal*
3.2.3   '−' : *Answer* ← *Answer* − *NextVal*
3.2.4   '*' : *Answer* ← *Answer* * *NextVal*
3.2.5   '/' : *Answer* ← *Answer*/*NextVal*
3.2.6 **else**
3.2.7   write out "Error! Enter last operator and number again."
3.2.8 **selectend**
3.3.1 write out "Enter operator or = to stop: "
3.3.2 read in *Operator*
4.1 **loopend when** *Operator* = '='
5.1.1 write out "The answer is ", *Answer*

At this stage it is a good idea to reflect on the design. Does it fulfil the demands of the specification? There are grey areas here. If you have worked with pocket calculators, you will appreciate that they do not give prompts for input and messages with final answers; it is assumed that the user is competent. There is no harm in including prompts and messages in this simulation.

Pocket calculators do give some output messages; they give error messages whenever they are unable to carry out a requested operation. One error trap has been built in: the default action in the **else** part detects any erroneous keypress when an operator is expected. Nothing has been done to ensure that, when requested to enter the next value, the user does enter a number rather than accidentally hitting some random key. Validation of user input is an important aspect of program design, and will be discussed in the next unit.

There is one further potential error which is worthy of mention at this stage. Step 3.2.5 defines the actions when division is selected. With division, one must always be careful to avoid dividing by zero. There is nothing in this design to prevent the user entering 0 as the value of the divisor following selection of the division operator. To get round this, step 3.2.5 could be refined as follows.

3.2.5.1   '/' : **if** $NextVal \neq 0$ **then**

3.2.5.2 $Answer \leftarrow Answer/NextVal$

3.2.5.3   **else**

3.2.5.4   write out "Cannot divide by 0. Last input ignored."

3.2.5.5   **ifend**

2.2 Coding the solution

In designing the solution, two constructs have been used for which the C++ implementation has not yet been introduced: the **when** loop and the **case** step. Let us investigate these two aspects before coding the design solution to the Calculator Simulation problem.

In C++ the design post-conditioned **when** loop (see page 10) codes as a **do while** loop. The structure, given below, is very similar to the pre-conditioned **while** loop, but with the control condition being after the loop body. The **do** is necessary as a marker to show where the loop body begins.

```
do
{
    statements of loop body;
}
while (condition);
```

There is one important point to remember in coding a design **when** step. Whereas the design of a post-conditioned loop can be read as 'stop looping when some condition becomes true', in C++ it is coded as 'keep looping while some condition remains true'. For example, the following design loop, in which *Mark* is a real variable,

1      $Mark \leftarrow 0$
2   **loop**
3   write out *Mark*
4        $Mark \leftarrow Mark + 0.8$
5   **loopend when** $Mark > 10$

codes as

```
Mark = 0;
do
{
  WriteFloat(Mark);
  Mark = Mark + 0.8;
}
while (Mark <= 10);
```

This code highlights similarities with the code for a pre-conditioned loop. As always in C++, the control condition is held in brackets. The loop body requires braces if it is a compound statement, but these braces may be omitted if it comprises a single statement. The braces are not followed by a semicolon.

High-level languages are evenly split on this feature. Some code the post-conditioned loop in the way that the design stage views it; others use the C++ approach.

The purpose of this design is to write out the values $0, 0.8, 1.6, 2.4, \ldots, 8.8, 9.6$.

Exercise 2.4 _____

Write C++ code corresponding to the following design fragment, in which _Total_ and _NextNumber_ are variables of integer type, and _MoreToCome_ is a character variable. Decide what is the purpose of this design, and include prompts when coding steps 3 and 5.

1   _Total_ ← 0
2   **loop**
3   read in _NextNumber_
4   _Total_ ← _Total_ + _NextNumber_
5   read in _MoreToCome_
6   **loopend when** _MoreToCome_ = 'N'

[_Solution on page 40_]

The design **case** step (see page 8) codes in C++ as a **switch** statement, the general form of which is as follows.

```
switch (expression)
{
  case constant1 : statement sequence; break;
  case constant2 : statement sequence; break;
    ... ;
  default : statement sequence;
}
```

The case labels, _constant1_, _constant2_, etc., are constant values of the same type. Suitable types are integer and any other types that are represented internally as integers. In this course, types meeting this requirement are given by `int`, `char` and `bool`. The control expression must evaluate to the same type as the case labels. If a match between the control expression and one of the case labels exists, then the corresponding statement sequence is executed until the **break** statement for that case is reached. The effect of **break** is to take the next instruction to be the one after the **switch** statement. (If a **break** keyword is omitted, the code in the case following the current one will also be executed. Sometimes this omission is a very useful feature; sometimes it leads to puzzling errors if you forget about the effect of the omission.) The action to be taken in each case is described as a statement sequence to emphasise that, in general, it will be a block of code; it may be many statements, a single statement, or indeed no statement at all (corresponding to 'do nothing').

The case labels must be presented as constants; they cannot be expressions which require evaluation.

When there is no match between the control expression and any of the case labels, the **default** case (corresponding to the **else** alternative in the design) is selected instead. There is no need for a **break** statement in the **default** case, since the next instruction _is_ the one after the **switch** statement. As in design, if the default statement sequence is 'do nothing', the **default** case is optional and may be omitted.

Finally, note that braces are not needed for _any_ of the statement sequences.

The following diagram indicates how the C++ **switch** statement works in various cases.

switch | case 1
case 2
case 3
default
next

switch | case 1
case 2
case 3
default
next

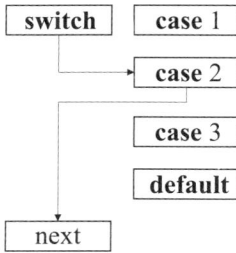

Case 2 matches, with **break** statement   Case 2 matches, no **break** statements

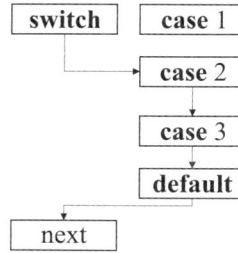

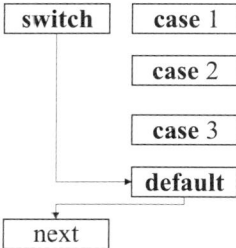

switch | case 1
case 2
case 3
default
next

switch | case 1
case 2
case 3
next

No case matches, with **default** statement   No case matches, no **default** statement

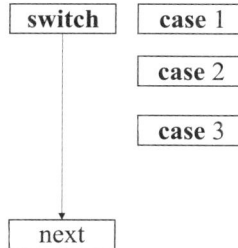

Below is a fragment of C^{++} code which demonstrates how a **switch** statement may be used in connection with a simple menu of choices. The user is invited to select from three options, and the **switch** is used to implement the appropriate actions depending on the value of a character variable, *Choice*, which is input by the user. The **default** part builds in a check for inadmissible inputs.

```
WriteStringCr("E:  Return to Edit.");
WriteStringCr("S:  Check spelling.");
WriteStringCr("Q:  Save File and Quit.");
Choice = ReadCharPr("Enter your choice: ");
switch (Choice)
{
  case 'E' : WriteString("E was selected.");
             break;
  case 'S' : WriteString("S was selected.");
             break;
  case 'Q' : WriteString("Q was selected.");
             break;
  default : WriteString("Choice not recognised");
}
```

The appendix 'Cr' on any of the Write instructions means that the write out is followed by a 'carriage return'; that is, subsequent writing will be on a new line of the screen. This appendix is not used with Read instructions.

The actions for the three cases merely report which option was selected. In a real application, the 'write out' statements would be replaced by the code to implement that selection. (Note that, in practice, the break statement for each case is usually placed on a separate line, as above.)

Exercise 2.5 ————————————————————

Suppose that the following fragment of C++ code, in which all variables concerned have been declared to be integers, is executed. (% is the remainder operator introduced in *Unit 2*, Subsection 2.2.)

```
Number = ReadIntPr("Enter number: ");
switch (Number % 5)
{
  case 0 : WriteString("Number is divisible by 5.");
           break;
  case 1 : WriteString("Good shot!");
           Hits = Hits + 1;
           break;
  default : Misses = Misses + 1;
}
```

What effect does the **switch** statement have when each of the following values is entered in response to the prompt for input?

(a) 14   (b) 15   (c) 16

Exercise 2.6 ————————————————————

Write a C++ **switch** statement to implement step 3.2 of the final design for the calculator simulation, including the refinement of step 3.2.5 which checked for division by 0.

[*Solutions on page 40*]

2.3 Implementing the solution

A final design for the Calculator Simulation problem now exists, and the C++ implementation of post-conditioned loops and selection has been discussed. The time has come to test the design by implementing the solution on your PC. Do not be impatient to start keying in code. At this stage of your development, it might be advisable to write the entire code on paper first. At least you should make notes to yourself regarding aspects of the translation of the design. What variables need to be declared, and what are their types? Which input and output functions are appropriate for use here? Are you happy with the translation of each design step into its equivalent C++ statement? Where are semicolons and braces needed?

When you are happy with your preparation, you can move on to implementing your solution in the practical activity that follows. Do not be surprised if your program fails to compile first time. Even experienced C++ programmers would anticipate the odd error creeping into the first attempt at a program of this size.

Computer Activity 2.1 _____

- ○ Start Builder and open a new console application.
- ○ Save the project in the `Block I` subfolder of `MT262`. (Use the names `CalcultrU` for the unit file and `Calcultr` for the project file.)
- ○ Use `Project|Add to Project...` to add `MT262io.lib`.
- ○ Add to the code template the statement

```
#include "MT262io.h"
```

to make the course library available, and the statement

```
getchar();
```

to hold the screen output.
- ○ Enter your code for the solution to the calculator simulation in the appropriate section of the template.
- ○ Run the program. If it fails to compile, try to decipher from the error messages generated what the errors are, and correct them.
- ○ When your program is running successfully, run it several times using data chosen to test the program.

Program testing is discussed more fully in *Unit 4*.

[*Solution on page 47*]

_____

This section has analysed the Calculator Simulation problem, and designed and coded a solution. In the course of doing so, the C++ implementations of **when** loops and **case** steps have been introduced.

3 Strings

If you have ever worked with a word-processing package, or received e-mail messages, or 'surfed' on the Internet, you will be aware of the importance in computing of handling textual material. The three examples mentioned are but a few of the numerous applications which involve storing, manipulating and displaying textual material in an appropriate format. The textual material referred to is more general than would be covered by the **string** data type (which was introduced in *Unit 2*), though there are similarities in that both are primarily concerned with strings of symbols from the set of characters. This section is the beginning of a more comprehensive study of the string data type.

3.1 Operations on strings

The six comparison operators for characters are applicable to the data type string, as follows. Two strings are equal (=) when they comprise exactly the same sequence of characters, in the same order. So, of the four strings "begin", "Begin", "□begin" and "begin□", no two are equal; for example "begin" ≠ "begin□". For the operators $<$, $\leq$, $>$ and $\geq$, string ordering is a generalisation of alphabetical ordering. That is, the order of two strings is determined, where possible, by the first characters of the strings; if the first characters are equal, the order is determined by the second characters; and so on. For example,

See *Unit 2*, Subsection 2.4.

The ASCII table is given in the Appendix to *Unit 2*.

"Seam" $<$ "Seat" — the first three characters are equal, but then 'm' $<$ 't';

"Seam" $<$ "Seams" — as would happen in alphabetical ordering;

"Seam□1" $<$ "Seam□2" — the first five characters are equal, but then '1' $<$ '2';

"Seam" $<$ "seam" — since 'S' $<$'s' in character order;

"□Seam" $<$ "Seam" — since '□' $<$ 'S' in character order.

The space character '□' is in position 32, coming before all the letters and digits.

Exercise 3.1

Mystring is a string variable with value "Dog". For each of the following (design) expressions, decide whether it is true or false.

(a) "alan" $<$ "Bob"

(b) *Mystring* $\leq$ "Cat"

(c) "D" $<$ *Mystring*

(d) "D□o□g" $\neq$ *Mystring*

(e) "Cat" $\geq$ "□"

[*Solution on page 41*]

In the same way that integer values can be assigned to real variables, character values can be assigned to string variables in C^{++}. That is, if *Str* is a string variable and *Ch* is an initialised character variable, then the assignment statement

```
Str = Ch;
```

is allowed, the value assigned to *Str* being a one-character string.

If 'a' is the value of *Ch*, then the value of *Str* under this assignment is "a".

The issue of what types of data can be assigned to what types of variable is usually fairly complicated in any actual language. Broadly, any given value can be assigned to a variable of a 'larger' type. You have seen an example of this: in the 'mean' problem in *Unit 2*, the compiler was forced to think of an **int** value as being a **float**. In the same way, assigning a **char** value to a string in C^{++} is reasonable (and allowed). The reverse assignments (**float** to **int** and string to **char**) are best avoided.

3.2 String indexes

The value "MY□FIRST□STRING" of the string variable *MyString* may be visualised as follows.

1	2	3	4	5	6	7	8	9	10	11	12	13	14	15
M	Y	□	F	I	R	S	T	□	S	T	R	I	N	G

At position 1 in the string there is character 'M', at position 2 there is character 'Y', ..., at position 15 there is character 'G'. These positions in the string (which hold characters) are called the **string indexes**. So 'M' is at index 1. 'Y' is at index 2, and 'G' is at index 15. The indexes of a string are referenced by putting the index in '[ ]' after the name of the string variable. So *MyString*[1] has current value 'M', *MyString*[2] has current value 'Y', and *MyString*[15] has current value 'G'. The idea of string indexes is an important one which will be used to update values of strings and to access individual characters within the string. For example, the assignment

$$MyString[11] \leftarrow \text{'P'}$$

changes the value at index 11, currently 'T', to 'P' and in so doing changes the value of *MyString* to "MY□FIRST□SPRING".

Exercise 3.2 _____

If *Str* is a string variable with value "ET□TU□BRUTE", what is the value of each of the following expressions?

(a) $Str[1]$

(b) $Str[6]$

(c) $Str[2] \neq Str[4]$

(d) $Str[2] = \text{'t'}$

[*Solution on page 41*]

One important attribute of a string value is its length, by which is meant the total number of characters making up that string. The constant strings "P", "Seam" and "MY□FIRST□STRING" have respective lengths 1, 4 and 15. The **null**, or **empty**, string, which we denote by "", has length 0 as it contains no characters. As the value of a string variable changes, so too does the length associated with that string variable. It is very useful to be able to refer to the length of a string variable: this is done by using the *Length* function, which applied to any string (variable or constant) gives the length of its current value. This is not an operation like the mathematical operations on reals and integers or the comparison operations, because it does not combine or compare two strings. Rather, it is applicable to a single string and returns an integer value. It is an example of a **function**, about which more will be said in Block II. In the meantime, there are some functions which will be used from the outset, and *Length* is one of them.

> The null string is *not* the same as the string "□" consisting of a single space character; the latter has length 1.

> Functions have names that conform to the same rules as names (identifiers) for variables.

The *Length* function is used in design steps such as the following three.

    $Size \leftarrow Length(Str) - 1$

    if $Length(Str) < 10$ **then** ...

    loop while $Count < Length(\text{"computing"})$

In the first of these examples, *Size* is an integer variable which is assigned value 1 less than the length of the current value of string variable *Str*. The variable to which the function is applied, *Str* in this case, is called the **argument** of the function *Length* in this expression. In the second example, the value of the *Length* function with *Str* again as argument is used in a condition. In the third example, a string constant is used as an argument for the *Length* function, as part of a condition.

Exercise 3.3

The string variables *Str1* and *Str2* have respective values "short" and "long". What are the values of the following expressions?

(a) *Length*(*Str1*)

(b) *Length*("□□")

(c) *Length*(*Str1*) − *Length*(*Str2*)

[*Solution on page 41*]

Warning

There is an important word of warning concerning string indexes. When the string variable *Str* has value "ET□TU□BRUTE", it has length 11. Therefore indexes from 1 to 11 may be used to refer to *Str*[1], *Str*[2], ..., *Str*[11]. Indexes outside the range 1 to 11 must not be used; for example, the identifier *Str*[14] has no value associated with it and is meaningless. Any attempt to access a non-existent position in a string will cause your program to fail. Your program *may* compile, but the operating system should recognise that you have tried to assign something to memory that does not 'belong' to your program. As part of its protection role, the operating system should trap this and cause your program to cease execution. (You might be trying to write over data belonging to a different program entirely.) So remember that the characters comprising a (non-null) string value occupy indexes from 1 to the length of the string, and be careful not to venture outside this range.

If, in the course of your practical work, you have seen a message box containing the word 'exception', then this was triggered by the protection part of the operating system.

In all the examples that you have met so far, string indexes have appeared as integer constants 1, 2, and so on. However, any expression which gives an integer value (in the correct range from 1 to the length of the string) may be used for an index. In particular, an integer variable may be used. For example, if *Next* is an initialised integer variable, then *Str*[*Next*] would identify the character in *Str* at index given by the current value of *Next*. As the value of *Next* varies, the value of *Str*[*Next*] varies accordingly.

In the exercise that follows, this idea is taken a little further: expressions which require evaluation are used as string indexes. It is important that indexes, and how to use them, so this exercise is an important one. If you answer all parts correctly, then you are well on the way to understanding indexes. If not, then do read the solution carefully, and make sure that you understand it before moving on.

Exercise 3.4 _____

If the string variable *Str* has value "Fundamentals" and *Next* is an integer
variable, what would be written out as a result of carrying out each of the
following design fragments?

(a) set *Next* to 3
    write out *Str*[*Next*]

(b) set *Next* to 4
    write out *Str*[2 * *Next* + 1]

(c) set *Next* to 3
    write out *Str*[4 * (*Next* + 1)]

(d) set *Next* to 6
    loop while *Next* < 12
        write out *Str*[*Next*]
        Next ← *Next* + 1
    loopend

(e) set *Next* to 6
    loop while *Next* > 3
        write out *Str*[*Next*]
        Next ← *Next* − 1
    loopend

[*Solution on page 42*]

_____

The operations on strings that have been discussed above will suffice for
the time being, and they are summarised in the table which follows. They
enable strings to be manipulated character by character. The *Length*
function can be used to ensure that no attempt is made to manipulate
non-existent characters of a string. In later units, further useful operations
on strings will be introduced, including ones for joining strings and
extracting parts of strings.

One point to note from the table is that the C++ word to declare a string
variable is **AnsiString**. This is *not* a keyword of C++, so it will not appear
emboldened when typed in a Builder Code Editor window. The reason for
this is that the C language (from which C++ was derived) did not support
a string data type; instead it treats strings as being built (in ways that you
will see in Blocks II and III) as collections of characters. The string type,
by way of *AnsiString* (provided by Builder), is a very useful addition to the
C++ language.

Design stage symbol	Meaning	C++ version
string	string	AnsiString
←	assignment	=
=	is equal to	==
≠	is not equal to	!=
<	is less than	<
>	is greater than	>
≤	is less than or equal to	<=
≥	is greater than or equal to	>=
MyString[*Index*]	character access (*Index* gives an integer value)	*MyString*[*Index*]
Length(*MyString*)	number of characters in string	(to be discussed later)

Strings are important because of the large amount of string data processed by computers. In non-embedded computer systems, string data probably represents the largest volume of data handled, although it is gradually being overtaken by data representing pictures and other graphic objects.

The idea of an instance of a data type (e.g. string) being made up of a sequence of instances of some other data type (e.g. character) will reappear in Block II, as will the use of an index to refer to individual items in the sequence. Thus the techniques that have been discussed for using indexes are useful more generally than just for string data.

In the next section, the ideas on string data are put to use.

4 Two problems

This section discusses two problems that involve the manipulation of strings, in particular investigating the characters that constitute a string. Solving the problems will involve the ideas about string indexes introduced in the previous section.

4.1 A first design

Here is the specification of the first problem.

Problem Specification   Word Counting

A program is required whose purpose is to receive a line of English text entered from the keyboard, and to write out the number of words in the text.   □

Is the problem clearly specified? There are a number of ambiguities that require clarification. What exactly is meant by 'a line of English text' and, within it, what exactly constitutes a word? For major software development, such questions require discussion with the client. To make progress, the course team will act as client and specify that the line will consist of letters, digits, punctuation symbols and space characters. Also, there is no requirement that a line should end with a full stop. Such a line can be represented by a string variable.

Words are normally identified by the presence of space characters surrounding them. The course team also specifies that, with the exception of the first and last words, each word consists of a sequence of non-space characters with a space character immediately before it and another immediately after it.

There are still ambiguities. The first word may or may not have a space character before it, and the last word may or may not have a space character following it. There is also the issue of multiple spaces: might there be more than one space character between words? Under the most liberal interpretation of the specification, all the following would be strings with four words.

"Hello!□This□is□MT262."

"Hello!□This□is□MT262.□"

"□□□Hello!□This□is□MT262.□□"

"Hello!□□□This□□is□MT262."

A string such as *I'll* and *time-keeper* will be counted as one word.

It is sensible to start by solving what ought to be the simplest case of the problem. You should assume that, as in the first illustration above, the input line must begin and end with non-space characters, and that there is just a single space between words. Taking decisions like this illustrates another aspect of the problem solving process: it is often advisable to begin by solving simple cases of the problem, with the objective of then adapting this first solution to cover more general cases. Here, when a program is written which successfully handles the restricted input lines, some reflection on what has been achieved may well enable a more general program to be produced by making minor modifications.

Now that *a* version of the problem has been fairly tightly specified, attention can be turned to a top-level design. To that end, you should think about this version of the the problem in general terms, with an eye on the 'input–process–output' model. The input is a line of text (i.e. characters), the words are to be counted, and the count is to be output. As can often be done, the top-level design can be given as three steps.

1   read in line of text
2   count words in line of text
3   write out count of words

A design decision has already been taken that all the input will be read in and then processed, rather than attempting to process the input character by character as it is typed.

In order to refine these steps, two things are needed. First, a preliminary data table (for variables) must be constructed. Secondly, a strategy for counting the words is required. The top-level design suggests two variables (and their types) that will be required, although the word-counting process may require others to be added later.

Exercise 4.1

Construct a data table describing two variables suggested by the top-level design.

Exercise 4.2

Suggest refinements of steps 1 and 3 that use the data table in the solution to Exercise 4.1. Include any prompts or text that you think are appropriate.

[*Solutions on page 42*]

Refining the remaining step (step 2 'count words in *Line*') is the heart of the problem. It is sometimes helpful with such problems to imagine how you could instruct someone at the other end of a telephone to carry out the process required. Before reading on, you might like to pause for a few minutes to think about such an imaginary telephone conversation.

The discussion on strings as indexed sequences of characters suggests that *Line* should be inspected character by character from start to end. Each new word encountered should increase the value of *WordCount* by 1. (There is also the possibility of counting ends of completed words, rather than starts of new ones. Both methods should give the same result.) Such a repetitious task is one for which a loop is ideally suited. To make this description more precise requires a decision on exactly how to recognise the start of a new word (or the end of a completed one). For the simplified problem that is being solved, since each space character is a marker between the end of one word and the start of the next, counting spaces provides a straightforward solution.

Recall that only one space is allowed between two consecutive words.

Exercise 4.3 ⎯⎯⎯⎯⎯⎯⎯⎯⎯⎯⎯⎯⎯

How is the number of words related to the number of spaces?

[*Solution on page 43*]

In order to inspect each character of *Line*, counting spaces on the way, two variables suggest themselves: an index variable for the string and a counter for the spaces, both integers. Adding these to the data table gives the following.

Type	Identifier	Description
String	*Line*	The line input by the user
Integer	*WordCount*	Count of the number of words found
Integer	*Index*	Index for characters in *Line*
Integer	*SpaceCount*	Count of space characters in *Line*

The refinement of step 2 that is suggested by all the above is as follows.

2.1   initialise any variables as necessary
2.2   **loop while** there are more characters in the line
2.3   process current character
2.4   **loopend**

The use of the word **while** here does not commit us to using a pre-conditioned loop: the design could be refined using a **when** loop. However, the **while** loop will be developed here. (Some discussion of the choice between the two types of conditioned loops is given in Block II.)

Since the loop is being used to examine each character in the line in turn, there will be one iteration per character. The index, *Index*, can be used to control the loop. On the first pass it has value 1, on the second value 2, and so on. The number of characters is not known in advance, but the length function which you met in Section 3 can be used to provide the number of characters in the string variable *Line*; it is *Length(Line)*. So on the final pass of the loop, *Index* will have value *Length(Line)*. The loop control given by

2.2   **loop while** $Index \leq Length(Line)$

is a reasonable choice.

In order for this loop to work correctly, *Index* must be initialised to an appropriate value and must be incremented by 1 somewhere in the loop body. The count of spaces, *SpaceCount*, must also be initialised.

28

Exercise 4.4

Refine step 2.1 to do the initialisation of *Index* and *SpaceCount*.

[Solution on page 43]

Finally, the body of the loop can be designed. The character currently being inspected is *Line*[*Index*], and this must be compared with the space character. If the current character is a space, then *SpaceCount* must be increased by 1; if not, nothing need be done. In either case, *Index* must then be incremented. After the loop, the value of *WordCount* must be set to *SpaceCount* + 1. A complete, final design based on this discussion is as follows.

1.1   write out "Enter a line of text. It may not start or end with a space, and words must be separated by a single space. It may not be empty."

1.2   read in *Line*

2.1.1 *Index* ← 1

2.1.2 *SpaceCount* ← 0

2.2   **loop while** *Index* ≤ *Length*(*Line*)

2.3.1   **if** *Line*[*Index*] = '□' **then**

2.3.2   *SpaceCount* ← *SpaceCount* + 1

2.3.3   **ifend**

2.3.4   *Index* ← *Index* + 1

2.4   **loopend**

2.5   *WordCount* ← *SpaceCount* + 1

3.1   write out "Number of words in text is ", *WordCount*

> The **if** step has no **else** part, so 'else do nothing' has been omitted.

You might have asked yourself whether both the variables *SpaceCount* and *WordCount* are needed. They are not; the two values that they represent are directly related. The design could be adapted to use either without the other. However, minimising the number of variables used is not necessarily an aim of a good program. It is certainly arguable that the algorithm used — count space characters and then add one to obtain the number of words — is more comprehensible when both variables are employed. One goal of a program is to keep the design (and consequently the code) comprehensible to a casual reader, and this sometimes implies using seemingly redundant variables for clarification purposes.

However, the simplicity of this design is a consequence of the relationship between the number of space characters and the number of words, which was, in turn, a consequence of the conditions imposed on the form of the user's input line. As those conditions are relaxed, the relationship will be lost and the word count process will become more complex.

The design above is a final design, in the sense that it is ready for coding in C++. Rather than coding *this* design, you are asked, in Subsection 4.3, to code the improved design introduced below.

4.2 Improving the solution

The design reached so far does solve the Word Counting problem subject to the constraints imposed on the input line. The prompt at step 1 spells out precisely the format of the line that the user must enter. But despite this prompt, the user cannot be relied upon to enter the string in this prescribed form, and a good program ought to check the format of the input line before proceeding. This is the area of 'data validation'; it will be looked at in *Unit 4*.

For now, a more ambitious plan is to consider dropping all the constraints on the input line. The definition of what constitutes a word will be retained, but the user will be allowed more freedom of the keyboard; space characters may appear in multiples, including at the start and end of the string. Rather than start the design process from scratch, the solution to the restricted problem will be adapted to this more general problem.

In the solution of the simplified version of the problem, the presence of words was recognised through the presence of space characters between words. After each space character, the next word is about to start. How can words be recognised in the more general lines which are now permitted? Essentially all that has changed is that 'single spaces between words' has been replaced by '(possibly) multiple spaces between words'.

The start of a new word is identified by the presence of a pair consisting of a space character followed immediately by a non-space character. This observation suggests a way of developing the earlier solution: instead of counting space characters, such pairs are counted. However, care must be taken with the start and end of the line, where things may be a little different. A line may start with no spaces, as in

This approach to counting words in a line means that there is no role for *SpaceCount* in the modified design.

"This□is□a□line□□with□no□initial□spaces."

or with one or more spaces, as in

"□□This□is□a□line□with□two□□initial□spaces."

The same is true of line endings.

"This□is□□a□line□with□no□final□□space."

"This□is□a□line□with□two□final□spaces.□□"

Some care is needed to ensure that all possibilities are dealt with, for both the start and the end of the input string.

The overall structure of the program will not change greatly from the simplified version; the processing will involve counting in a different way, and no doubt different initialisations will be required, but the same top-level design should fit the bill. The following first refinement of that design may thus be written down. Note that the prompt for the user can be quite simple, as there are fewer restrictions.

1.1   write out "Enter a non-empty line of text: "
1.2   read in *Line*
2.1   initialise variables
2.2   count words in *Line*
3.1   write out "Number of words in text is ", *WordCount*

The method of scanning along *Line* using *Index* to mark the current position can be used again. This time, there is an additional complication: not only do we have to inspect the current character, *Line*[*Index*], we also have to 'remember' the previous one. When the previous character is a space and the current one is not a space, the start of another word has been found. An additional variable, *Previous*, of character type, will be needed to hold the value of the previous character. The value of *Previous* will be the previous value of *Line*[*Index*]. Hence, just before increasing *Index* by 1 (to move on to the next character), the value of *Previous* will need to be updated.

The subtasks of step 2.2, the loop body, are to update the value of *WordCount* (add 1 or not, as the case may be), to keep track of *Previous* and to increment *Index* to the next value.

Exercise 4.5

Construct an updated data table.

Exercise 4.6

Suggest a suitable loop condition and initial values for *Index* and *Previous*. Incorporate these decisions into a refinement of step 2.2. In setting up the initial value for *Previous*, be careful to ensure that the first word in *Line* will be counted.
(Do not spend too long on this. If you are not sure how to proceed, read the text preceding the design given in the solution and have another go.)

[*Solutions on page 43*]

The final stage is to finish the processing of the current character. As already discussed, if the current character is a non-space *and* the previous one is a space, then *WordCount* should be increased by 1. This suggests the following design.

1.1 write out "Enter a non-empty line of text: "
1.2 read in *Line*
2.1.1 *Index* ← 1
2.1.2 *Previous* ← '□'
2.1.3 *WordCount* ← 0
2.2.1 **loop while** *Index* ≤ *Length*(*Line*)
2.2.2 **if** (*Previous* = '□') **and** (*Line*[*Index*] ≠ '□') **then**
2.2.3   *WordCount* ← *WordCount* + 1
2.2.4 **ifend**
2.2.5 *Previous* ← *Line*[*Index*]
2.2.6 *Index* ← *Index* + 1
2.2.7 **loopend**
3.1 write out "Number of words in text is ", *WordCount*

4.3 Testing the solution

There are good grounds for feeling reasonably confident that this design for the general Word Counting problem will function correctly, but the acid test comes when the program is coded and run. It is quite ambitious to give no constraints at all on the input line, and the program will need to be tested carefully.

You may be tempted to switch on your computer and key in the program, working from the above design. The course team hopes you will, indeed, acquire such confidence before too long. However, the translation from design to code still holds many pitfalls, and the course team advice is that you plan your coding on paper before going to the machine. Hence the coding is first posed as a 'pencil and paper' exercise.

There is one element of this coding which you have not been told about as yet: the function *Length*. The `MT262io` library contains a suitable function called *Length*. Thus the loop condition is coded as follows.

```
while (Index <= Length(Line))
```

Exercise 4.7
Translate the design for the Word Counting problem into C++ code.

[*Solution on page 44*]

When you are happy that you have all the coding issues resolved you can turn to running it on your computer.

Computer Activity 4.1
Start Builder and open a new console application. Save the unit as `WCountU` and save the project as `WCount` in the **Block I** subfolder of `MT262`. Add to the provided code template the statements to make the course library MT262io available and to hold the screen output. Enter your code for the Word Counting problem. Run the program, correcting any compilation errors that occur.

You will need to add `MT262io.lib` to the project and to add an `#include` statement.

When your program has compiled correctly, test that it functions properly by entering each of the following strings in response to the prompt.

(a) The string "□□Testing□the□□□design"

(b) The string "Testing□the□□□design□□"

(c) The string "Abracadabra", containing no space characters

(d) The empty string (which is entered by pressing **Enter**)

(e) The string "□□□□" consisting of space characters alone

(f) The string "The□,□boy"

[*Solution on page 47*]

The prompt asked the user not to enter the empty string. Nevertheless, it is sensible to check that the program does not fall over if the empty string *is* entered.

The six test strings were carefully chosen to cover the various aspects of the program. The first two cover the acceptance of multiple spaces. The strings in (c)–(e) test 'extreme cases', namely no space characters present, the empty string, and no non-space characters present. Although the program caters for these cases successfully, it is such extremes that are most useful when searching for design flaws. The last case illustrates that the earlier discussion of what constitutes a word is incomplete — this matter will be taken no further here.

Testing designs, and implemented code, is an important feature of problem solving that is looked at in more detail in *Unit 4*.

4.4   An extension problem

To round off the section, a variation on the Word Counting problem is posed that will provide you with the opportunity to practise using string indexes and will introduce some slightly different aspects to the problem of searching strings. Instead of counting words in a given line, your revised task is to write out the first word in the line.

Problem Specification   First Word

A program is required in which the user enters a line of English text from the keyboard, and the first word in that line is written to the screen.   □

As with the Word Counting problem, there are ambiguities in this specification. The same decisions concerning what constitutes a word will be made as for the Word Counting problem. In addition, you may assume, for an initial solution, that the user enters at least one word — that is, at least one non-space character. Catering for extreme cases will be considered in due course. A top-level design, with no detail, could be as follows.

1   get input line from user
2   find first word
3   write out word

Exercise 4.8 _____

Using your experience of the Word Counting problem, suggest a suitable data table.

Exercise 4.9 _____

Refine step 1 in the top-level design.

Exercise 4.10 _____

Describe, in words, how to find the beginning of the first word.

Exercise 4.11 _____

Describe, in words, how to find the end of the first word.

[Solutions on page 44]

The use of the scanning approach discussed in the solutions to Exercises 4.10 and 4.11 suggests that separating finding the first word from writing it out (steps 2 and 3) may not have been such a wise decision. It is slightly simpler to write out the characters of the first word as they are scanned (stopping when the end of the word is found). Thus the writing out should be inside whatever loop is used to scan the string. Actually, the various points discussed in these solutions indicate that there will be two loops: one to scan up to the start of the first word, and another to scan until the end of this word is reached. Thus a modified and refined design, incorporating only the second of these loops, is as follows.

1.1   write out "Enter a non-empty line of text: "

1.2   read in *Line*

2.1   find start of first word

3.1   **loop while** still in first word

3.2   write out current character

3.3   **loopend**

Before reaching the 'ready for coding' stage, two things need to be done to the above design: step 2.1 must be refined, and the loop condition in step 3.1 needs some careful consideration.

Exercise 4.12

Using the solution to Exercise 4.10 as a basis, refine step 2.1 using a suitable **while** loop. You may find it helpful to check that your solution would handle the inputs "□□first" and "first" correctly.

Exercise 4.13

Describe a suitable loop condition for step 3.1. You should check that your suggestion would handle the inputs "spaces□□" and "nospaces" correctly.

Exercise 4.14

Using the solutions to Exercises 4.12 and 4.13 as a basis, refine the above design to a stage where it is ready for coding into C++. Are there any 'extreme' cases of input that your solution will not handle correctly?

[*Solutions on page 45*]

The refinement of step 3 using a **while** loop will be pursued here, but a **when** loop is equally appropriate.

How should the problem of a user who ignores the instruction to enter a *non-empty* line of text be dealt with? There are two common approaches: to modify the design to accept an empty input line, *or* to modify it so that the user is repeatedly asked for acceptable input. In any particular application, these two approaches have to be considered carefully. If it is vital that the user provides input, then there is no choice — the latter (dictatorial) modification has to be done. In other cases, the danger is of annoying the user. Here, as 'the client', the course team asks you to adopt the second approach and reject entry of the empty string.

Exercise 4.15

Modify the design so that it copes with both the 'all spaces' problem and the 'empty line' problem described above.

[*Solution on page 46*]

The final activity asks you to code the final design from the solution to Exercise 4.15.

Computer Activity 4.2 ───────────────────

Code the design in the solution to Exercise 4.15. You will need a new console application, and you will have to make the course library available in the usual way. It is suggested that you save the unit as `FstWrdU` and save the project as `FstWrd` in the `Block I` subfolder of `MT262`. Run and test your code.

[*Solution on page 47*]

───

In the two problems tackled in this section, the issue of dealing with possible errors has already absorbed a significant amount of effort. Two specific types of error have been considered at the design stage. The possibility of running 'off the end' of an input string was dealt with by careful construction of loop conditions. The input of an empty line was also dealt with by a loop.

The various types of error that can occur during design, coding and use are discussed in the next unit. However, you may already feel that dealing with errors and extreme cases can obscure the basic simplicity of a design. This is a real problem in software development in that it sometimes leads to skimping, particularly on the trapping of user errors. A partial solution lies in splitting designs and code into separate chunks, called **modules**. With this approach, the trapping of errors can be addressed separately, with the result that it becomes a task in its own right and not a distraction from the main purpose of the design or program. Block II will introduce and use ideas of modular design and coding.

Objectives

After studying this unit, you should be able to:

o   design solutions for simple problems that involve pre-conditioned
   while loops;

o   design solutions for simple problems that involve post-conditioned
   when loops;

o   design solutions for simple problems that involve **case** steps;

o   include elementary trapping of user errors in your designs;

o   code designs that use **while**, **when** and/or **case** constructs;

o   use string variables, and operations on them;

o   use the notion of an index to access the individual entries that make up
   a string;

o   complete a program from a coded design, including ensuring that the
   course library is included in your project;

o   show, in problem solving, an appreciation of the 'specify, design and
   refine, code, test' process;

o   use and understand the use of the following terms: sequence, selection,
   selector, case step, case label, iteration, conditioned loop, while loop,
   when loop, pre-conditioned loop, post-conditioned loop, string,
   null or empty string, function, argument of a function.

Solutions to the Exercises

Section 1

Solution 1.1
A completed design is as follows.

> **if** lights are red **then**
>> stop
>
> **else**
>> **if** lights are green **then**
>>> go
>>
>> **else**
>>> **if** lights are amber **then**
>>>> stop if safe
>>>
>>> **else**
>>>> prepare to go
>>>
>>> **ifend**
>>
>> **ifend**
>
> **ifend**

'lights are red' means 'lights are red only'.

This else step covers the 'red and amber ' case.

Solution 1.2
The first missing statement has to cover the case where the car *is* a saloon but the driver is 25 or over: the premium has to be set to 290. The other missing section has to deal with *both* remaining age cases for cars which are sports cars (i.e not saloons). One solution is as follows.

> **if** type of car is saloon **then**
>> **if** age of driver is under 25 **then**
>>> *Premium* ← 360
>>
>> **else**
>>> *Premium* ← 290
>>
>> **ifend**
>
> **else**
>> **if** age of driver is under 25 **then**
>>> *Premium* ← 520
>>
>> **else**
>>> *Premium* ← 440
>>
>> **ifend**
>
> **ifend**

Solution 1.3

A completed is as follows.

> read in next character from keyboard
>
> **select case** depending on character
>> 'a': add 1 to count of a's
>>
>> 'e': add 1 to count of e's
>>
>> 'i': add 1 to count of i's
>>
>> 'o': add 1 to count of o's
>>
>> 'u': add 1 to count of u's
>
> **else**
>> add 1 to count of non-vowels
>
> **selectend**

Solution 1.4

The pre-conditioned loop would have the following form.

> initialise *NextChar*
>
> **loop while** *NextChar* does not lie in range 'A' to 'Z'
>> write out "Enter a character: "
>>
>> read in *NextChar*
>
> **loopend**

The two loops are more or less the same, except that the pre-condition used here is the negation of the post-condition used in the corresponding **when** loop. The initialisation for the pre-conditioned loop is important: before the control step is encountered, *NextChar* must already be initialised, for otherwise the condition cannot be evaluated. The post-conditioned loop does not need this, because *NextChar* is given a value inside the loop body *before* the condition is evaluated for the first time.

Another difference is covered in the main text.

Solution 1.5

The number that is read in is initially assigned to both *First* and *Next*. On each pass of the loop — and there is certainly one pass because the loop is post-conditioned — the current value of *Next* is written out and then it is changed. If *Next* has an odd value, it is multiplied by 3 and then 1 is subtracted. On the other hand when the value of *Next* is even, it is updated by being halved. Looping stops when the value of *Next* is less than or equal to its original value.

(a) Tracing this when the original value is 5 gives:

> on first iteration, 5 is written out and *Next* becomes 14;
>
> on second iteration, 14 is written out and *Next* becomes 7;
>
> on third iteration, 7 is written out and *Next* becomes 20;
>
> on fourth iteration, 20 is written out and *Next* becomes 10;
>
> on fifth iteration, 10 is written out and *Next* becomes 5.

The control condition now stops the loop.

(b) When the initial value is 6, the first iteration writes out 6 and updates *Next* to 3, which stops the loop. So just 6 is written out.

(c) When the initial value is 9, the following numbers are written out:

> $9, 26, 13, 38, 19, 56, 28, 14.$

Section 2

Solution 2.1

As the calculation progresses, there is one amount, the 'answer so far', that keeps changing as further operations take place on it. Its final value will be the answer required. As the values are in general real, a real variable with identifier *Answer*, say, is suitable for this purpose. Two further variables are needed for the two user inputs at each stage: an operator and a value. The operator will be applied to the two operands, namely the current value of *Answer* and the value entered after the operator. The latter value may be a whole number but, for generality, it can be assumed to be real. So the value entered from the keyboard can be held by a variable of type real, with identifier *NextVal*, say.

The operator has five values, '+', '−', '*', '/' and '=', which are characters. So to read in the operator for the next part of the calculation, a character variable with identifier *Operator*, say, will be used.

Here is the provisional data table. Other variables may need to be added as the design is refined.

Type	Identifier	Description
Real	*Answer*	Current answer to the on-going calculation
Character	*Operator*	The operator used at next stage, or '=' to stop
Real	*NextVal*	Number read in to be associated with *Operator*

Solution 2.2

In fact, any one of the four alternatives could be refined to a successful solution of this problem. It does not matter in this instance whether a pre-conditioned or a post-conditioned loop is chosen. Step 1 is still entirely unspecified, so the variables can be initialised as required for either form of loop. In other situations where a loop is required in which variables are already initialised, the choice of a pre-conditioned or a post-conditioned loop could matter — but not here.

There is one feature which does influence the choice. Suppose that (a) or (b) is chosen. In each case, the first thing to occur in the loop body is that an *Operator* is read in. What happens if this is '='? In such an event, the loop should be left immediately, with no values being read in or processed. This means that some form of selection would have to be built into the loop body: **if** '=' is entered do one thing, **else** do something different. This need for selection can be avoided in (c) and (d), where reading in *Operator* is the final action in the loop body. In these cases, if *Operator* = '=', then the loop is exited immediately. Overall, (c) and (d) look like leading to the neatest solutions.

Solution 2.3

There are valid alternative approaches to the refinement of step 1 that is given below. For instance, a simple, and perfectly acceptable, solution just reads in the initial values of *NextVal* and *Operator* as step 1. If your solution followed this route, then you are thinking on sound lines. However, the course team solution sets *Answer* to 0 and *Operator* to '+'. Notice the effect of this in the first execution of the loop: the first value read in (at step 3.1) is added to 0 (at step 3.2) to become the value of *Answer*.

1.1   *Answer* ← 0
1.2   *Operator* ← '+'
2.1   **loop**
3.1   read in *NextVal*
3.2   update *Answer*
3.3   read in *Operator*
4.1   **loopend when** *Operator* = '='
5.1   write out *Answer*

Note once again that there is no such thing as *the* correct answer; design involves individual choice. The course team solution was influenced by the fact that most calculators display the number 0 when first switched on; but the problem specification does not imply that *Answer* must originally be 0. That was a choice made.

Solution 2.4

The design is adding integer values entered from the keyboard. After the first and each subsequent number, the user presses a key to indicate that there is more to come. The key 'N' denotes the end of input (as in the design), and the key 'Y' has been used to indicate 'more input to come'.

```
Total = 0;
do
{
  NextNumber = ReadIntPr("Enter number: ");
  Total = Total + NextNumber;
  MoreToCome = ReadCharPr("Any more? Type Y (yes) or N (no).");
}
while (MoreToCome != 'N');
```

Solution 2.5

The control expression is *Number* % 5, which is the remainder on dividing *Number* by 5.

(a) When 14 is entered as the value of *Number*, the control expression evaluates to 4, this being the remainder on dividing 14 by 5. As 4 does not match any of the **case** labels, the default action is executed, resulting in the value of *Misses* being increased by 1.

(b) When *Number* is 15, the control expression evaluates to 0, which matches the first **case** label. As a result, the string "Number is divisible by 5." is written to the screen.

(c) When *Number* is 16, the control expression evaluates to 1, which matches the second **case** label. As a result, the string "Good shot!" is written to the screen, and the value of *Hits* is increased by 1.

Solution 2.6

```
switch (Operator)
{
  case '+' : Answer = Answer + NextVal;
             break;
  case '-' : Answer = Answer - NextVal;
             break;
  case '*' : Answer = Answer * NextVal;
             break;
  case '/' : if (NextVal != 0)
                    Answer = Answer/NextVal;
             else
                    WriteStringCr("Cannot divide by 0. Last input ignored.");
             break;
  default : WriteStringCr("Error! Enter last operator and number again.");
}
```

Section 3

Solution 3.1

(a) False, since 'a' > 'B'. The upper-case letters precede the lower-case ones in character order. (The ASCII table is given in the Appendix to *Unit 2*.)

(b) False, since 'D' > 'C'. ('D' is the first character of "Dog", the value of *Mystring*.)

(c) True.

(d) True, since a string of 5 characters cannot be equal to a string of 3 characters. (In fact, as the space character comes before 'o' in ASCII order, "D☐o☐g" < "Dog".)

(e) True, since 'C' > '☐'.

Solution 3.2

(a) The character 'E'.

(b) The space character '☐'.

(c) False. Both sides of the comparison are equal to the character 'T', so equality holds.

(d) False. *Str*[2] has the value 'T', and this is not the same character as 't'.

Solution 3.3

(a) 5

(b) 2

(c) 1

Solution 3.4

(a) The character at index 3, namely 'n', is written out.

(b) When *Next* has value 4, 2 * *Next* + 1 has value 9, so the character at index 9, namely 't', is written out.

(c) When *Next* has value 3, 4 * (*Next* + 1) has value 16. This is *out of range*. The current value of *Str* has length 12, so any attempt to access a character with index outside the range 1 to 12 at this time is an error.

(d) *Next* starts with value 6. At each pass of the loop, the character at the index given by *Next* is written out, and *Next* is increased by 1. So during the first pass, *Str*[6] is written out (that is, the character 'm') and *Next* increases to 7. Then *Str*[7] is written out and *Next* increases to 8. This continues until *Str*[11] is written out and *Next* increases to 12. As this point, the loop terminates. So the characters at indexes 6 to 11 inclusive in *Str* are written out one after another. That is, the six characters forming the string "mental" are written out.

(It is assumed that the characters are written out at consecutive positions on the same line, rather than (say) each on a new line. When implementation is considered, ways of controlling such output should also be dealt with. The important thing for this problem is to appreciate which six letters are written out.)

(e) Each time the loop body is executed, the value of *Next* is reduced by 1. As *Next* is initialised to 6, the loop executes with *Next* having values 6, then 5, and then 4. When *Next* reaches 3, the loop condition is false and iteration finishes. It follows that what will be written out is *Str*[6] on the first pass, followed by *Str*[5] on the second pass, and *Str*[4] on the third and final pass. In all, the string "mad" is written out.

Section 4

Solution 4.1

To store the input line entered by the user, a string variable is required; *Line* is a reasonable identifier. Since the output will be an integer representing the word count, *WordCount* will be used for this variable. The initial data table is as follows.

Type	Identifier	Description
String	*Line*	The line input by the user
Integer	*WordCount*	Count of the number of words found

Until the counting strategy has been formulated, this is as far as the table can be taken.

Solution 4.2
The design given here includes a lengthy prompt that explains the restrictions on the text to be input.

1.1   write out "Enter a line of text. It may not start or end with a space, and words must be separated by a single space. It may not be empty."
1.2   read in *Line*
2   count words in *Line*
3.1   write out "Number of words in text is ", *WordCount*

(Note that a single space follows 'is' in step 3.1, in order to produce well-spaced output. Also note that step 2 has been recast, using the variable name, rather than refined.)

Solution 4.3
There is one more word than the number of spaces, because there is no space at the start or the end of *Line*.

Solution 4.4
The first character in a string is at index (in position) 1. The initial number of spaces is 0.

2.1.1 *Index* ← 1
2.1.2 *SpaceCount* ← 0

Solution 4.5
Note that, as previously stated, there is no role for *SpaceCount* in the new scenario. The new variable *Previous* has to be added.

Type	Identifier	Description
String	*Line*	The line input by the user
Integer	*WordCount*	Count of the number of words found
Integer	*Index*	Index for characters in *Line*
Character	*Previous*	Previous character for comparison

Solution 4.6
The loop can be controlled in exactly the same way as for the first solution. Initialising *Index* is straightforward: it must start at 1 (and end at *Length(Line)*). However, *Previous* needs a little thought. To begin with (when *Index* is 1), there is no previous character, so *Previous* must be given an artificial value. Suppose for a moment that *Line*[1] is not a space character, so that a word starts immediately. Since the test for the start of a word is that a non-space character is found when *Previous* is a space, the only way the start of the first word will be recognised is by setting *Previous* to '□'. Imagining a space at the beginning of any input string does not alter the number of words, so setting *Previous* to '□' is essential.

2.1.1 *Index* ← 1
2.1.2 *Previous* ← '□'
2.1.3 *WordCount* ← 0
2.2.1 **loop while** *Index* ≤ *Length(Line)*
2.2.2   process current character
2.2.3 **loopend**

Solution 4.7

```
AnsiString Line;
int Index;
int WordCount;
char Previous;
  Line = ReadStringPr("Enter a non-empty line of text: ");
  Index = 1;
  Previous = ' ';
  WordCount = 0;
  while (Index <= Length(Line))
  {
   if ((Previous == ' ') && (Line[Index] != ' '))
     WordCount = WordCount + 1;
   Previous = Line[Index];
   Index = Index + 1;
  }
  WriteIntPrCr("Number of words in text is ", WordCount);
```

Solution 4.8

A string variable will be required for the input from the user. It also seems likely that an integer variable will be useful as an index. An initial data table is as follows.

Type	Identifier	Description
String	*Line*	Input from user
Integer	*Index*	Index variable for use with *Line*

Solution 4.9

For the task to make sense, the line of input ought to be non-empty, so the prompt to the user should say so.

1.1 write out "Enter a non-empty line of text: "
1.2 read in *Line*

Solution 4.10

Scan the characters in *Line* until the first non-space character is found. The first non-space character is the start of the first word.

Solution 4.11

A first suggestion might be that the first space found after finding the start of the first word will mark the end of that word. However, there is always the possibility that the user enters just one word, with no trailing space. A safe procedure is: scan the characters from the start of the first word until a space is found *or* the end of *Line* is reached.

Note that the strategies in this solution and the previous one will not handle input from a user who insists on entering an empty string.

Solution 4.12

Scanning the characters in *Line* for a non-space character means starting with *Index* set to 1 (the start of the line), testing *Line*[*Index*] to see if it is a space and increasing *Index* by 1 if it is. This suggests that a suitable loop condition is *Line*[*Index*] = '□'. Thus a refinement of step 2.1 is as follows.

2.1.1 *Index* ← 1
2.1.2 **loop while** *Line*[*Index*] = '□'
2.1.3   *Index* ← *Index* + 1
2.1.4 **loopend**

When the loop stops executing, *Index* will be such that *Line*[*Index*] is the first non-space character in *Line*. Because a pre-conditioned loop has been used, "first" (with no leading space(s)) will be handled correctly. *Line*[1] will be tested and found to be a non-space character, and the loop will not be executed at all. For "□□first", the loop will execute twice, so that *Index* is increased to 3. At this point *Line*[*Index*] is not a space, and the loop stops.

Solution 4.13

Earlier discussion suggests that the loop condition must have two parts: checking for a space and for the end of the input string. A suitable condition is the following.

  (*Index* ≤ *Length*(*Line*)) **and** (*Line*[*Index*] ≠ '□')

The "spaces□□" case will be handled by the second part of the loop condition (and *Index* will be 7 when the loop exits). The "nospaces" case will be terminated by the first part of the loop condition, with *Index* set to 9, one more than the length of this string.

Solution 4.14

Putting the various pieces together yields the following design.

1.1   write out "Enter a non-empty line of text: "
1.2   read in *Line*
2.1.1 *Index* ← 1
2.1.2 **loop while** *Line*[*Index*] = '□'
2.1.3   *Index* ← *Index* + 1
2.1.4 **loopend**
3.1   **loop while** (*Index* ≤ *Length*(*Line*)) **and** (*Line*[*Index*] ≠ '□')
3.2.1   write out *Line*[*Index*]
3.2.2   *Index* ← *Index* + 1
3.3   **loopend**

There are two problems left. One is that an input consisting entirely of spaces will cause an error in the loop that searches for the start of the first word: *Index* will run 'off the end' of *Line* (that is, *Index* will end up greater than *Length*(*Line*)). The other is that an empty input line is not dealt with. In this case, *Line*[1], which is required in the condition in step 2.1.2, does not exist!

Solution 4.15

The 'all spaces' problem can be dealt with by using the condition
$Index \leq Length(Line)$, in steps 2.1.2 and 3.1 below, and issuing an
appropriate message, in step 3.5.2. If an 'all spaces' line is input, $Index$ will
be incremented at step 2.1.3 (in the loop designed to find the start of the
first word) until it exceeds $Length(Line)$, at which point the loop condition
in step 2.1.2 becomes false, and execution then passes to step 3.1. Since the
condition in this step is false, the following loop (which is designed to
identify the end of the first word) is not entered, and execution passes to
step 3.5.2 (the message).

The second problem requires a personal decision about how to inform the
user that a mistake has been made. The design below just produces a
message (in step 1.2.3) to the effect that the input was not as expected.
Note that the presence of step 1.2.4 means that the first loop cannot be
exited until the user provides an acceptable line.

1.1   write out "Enter a non-empty line of text: "

1.2.1 read in $Line$

1.2.2 **loop while** $Line = $ ""

1.2.3   write out "Please enter a non-empty line."

1.2.4   read in $Line$

1.2.5 **loopend**

2.1.1 $Index \leftarrow 1$

2.1.2 **loop while** $(Index \leq Length(Line))$ **and** $(Line[Index] = \text{'}\square\text{'})$

2.1.3 $Index \leftarrow Index + 1$

2.1.4 **loopend**

3.1   **if** $Index \leq Length(Line)$ **then**

3.2   **loop while** $(Index \leq Length(Line))$ **and** $(Line[Index] \neq \text{'}\square\text{'})$

3.3.1   write out $Line[Index]$

3.3.2 $Index \leftarrow Index + 1$

3.4   **loopend**

3.5.1 **else**

3.5.2   write out "You have entered a line with all spaces."

3.6   **ifend**

Since this design is a
modification rather than a
refinement of the earlier one,
the step numbering reflects
this.